THE TREMBLING EARTH

Written by John Dudman
Illustrated by Julian Baker

CollinsEducational
An Imprint of HarperCollinsPublishers

Contents

Introduction

It would be easy to believe that the Earth never changes. In fact, the surface of our planet is constantly on the move.

The immense power of the centre of the Earth has not only created land, mountains and oceans, but has moved them around the globe. These powers can be seen today when earthquakes strike and volcanoes erupt, causing terrifying disasters which destroy and reshape parts of our world.

The air and moisture in the Earth's atmosphere is what keeps us alive — but the huge storms which can suddenly blow from tropical seas have enormous and dangerous power. They can flatten towns, killing many people, and have the strength to wipe out ancient forests and even alter coastlines.

This book is an introduction to the power of our amazing planet, and explains the causes and consequences of the natural disasters which affect so many people around the world.

In the beginning ...

No-one knows precisely how the Earth began. Throughout history, people have been arguing about the origins of the world. Modern scientists believe that it was created along with the Sun and the other planets from a huge cloud of dust, 4,560 million years ago. The dust formed larger and larger particles which eventually gathered together to form Earth and the other planets in our solar system.

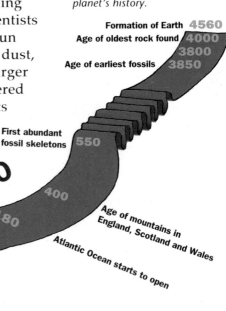

▼ This timeline shows that humans have been on Earth for only a tiny fraction of the planet's history.

Formation of Earth **4560**
Age of oldest rock found **4000**
3800
Age of earliest fossils **3850**

First abundant fossil skeletons **550**

MILLIONS OF YEARS AGO

400

180

Age of mountains in England, Scotland and Wales

Atlantic Ocean starts to open

65

Extinction of dinosaurs

30 Age of Alps

2 First humans

Inside the Earth

The Earth is made up of layers, rather like an onion.

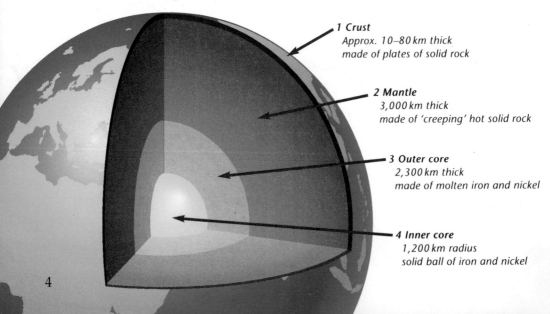

1 Crust
Approx. 10–80 km thick made of plates of solid rock

2 Mantle
3,000 km thick made of 'creeping' hot solid rock

3 Outer core
2,300 km thick made of molten iron and nickel

4 Inner core
1,200 km radius solid ball of iron and nickel

You don't have to go very far into the Earth's crust to feel the heat of the mantle. Temperatures are very high deep down in mines: three kilometres down, the rock is 70°C, the temperature of a very hot radiator. Nine kilometres deep, temperatures of 300°C, three times as hot as boiling water, have been measured.

The changing surface

We live on top of the Earth's crust. The crust is not one unbroken shell, but is made up of 12 giant **crustal plates**. The plates rest on the Earth's mantle. The mantle is made of extremely hot solid rock. It is close to its melting point, and it stretches rather like very hot thick toffee. The currents of heat make it 'creep' or flow slowly. The rock moves at about the same speed as fingernails grow: a few centimetres a year. The currents of heat circulating slowly within the mantle cause the plates to move against one another. This process of movement is called **plate tectonics**.

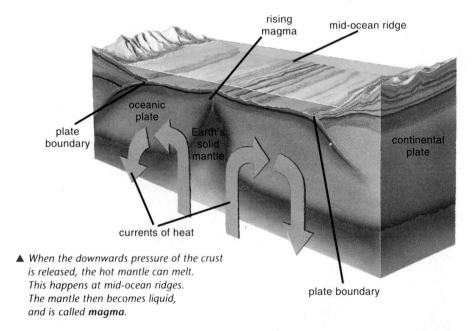

▲ When the downwards pressure of the crust is released, the hot mantle can melt. This happens at mid-ocean ridges. The mantle then becomes liquid, and is called **magma**.

The movement of the plates seems very slow. For example, the gap between the plates in the Atlantic Ocean widens by one to five centimetres a year. But this means that over a century, London becomes five metres further away from New York, and New York becomes 18 metres closer to Tokyo!

Continental movements

The position of the continents we live on today is very different from how it was when the Earth began.

▶ *South America and Africa were linked. India had been attached to Antarctica, but moved north to join Asia. Australia had been part of Antarctica. There were only two great oceans: the Pacific (which was a very different shape than it is today) and the Tethys, which separated Africa from Asia.*

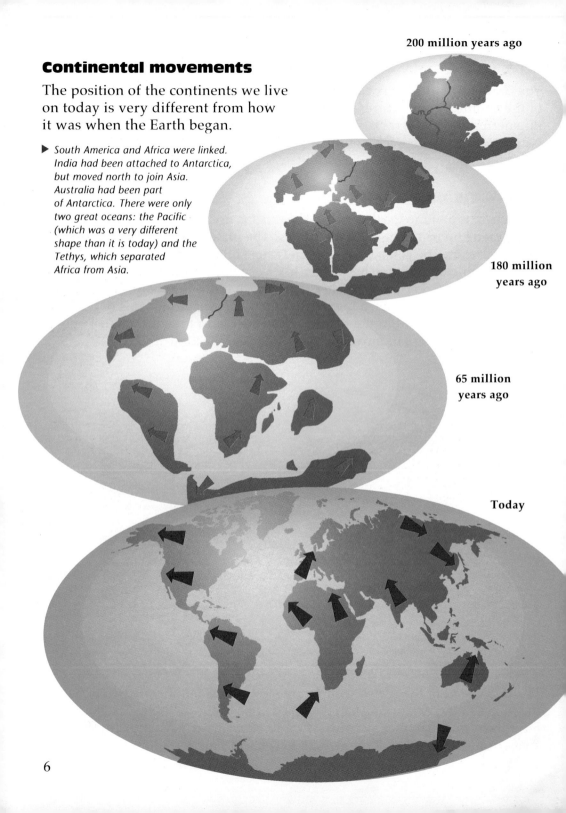

200 million years ago

180 million years ago

65 million years ago

Today

6

The position and shapes of the continents will continue to change. Scientists have used computers to predict the movements of the Earth over the next 250 million years. Their predictions are based on knowledge of the speed and direction in which the plates are travelling. They estimate that Africa will edge north, replacing the Mediterranean Sea with a new mountain range. Australia will also move north towards Indonesia. California will split and move away from the US mainland.

The changing position of Antartica

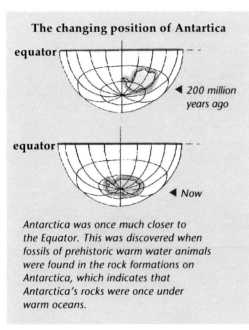

Antarctica was once much closer to the Equator. This was discovered when fossils of prehistoric warm water animals were found in the rock formations on Antarctica, which indicates that Antarctica's rocks were once under warm oceans.

The growing mountain

Mount Everest is the tallest mountain in the world. But it is made of marine limestone rock, which scientists say proves that it was once part of the sea bed. And Everest is still changing. Towering 8,848 metres above the Himalayan nation of Nepal, it is today 23 centimetres higher than it was in 1959!

Moving marsupials

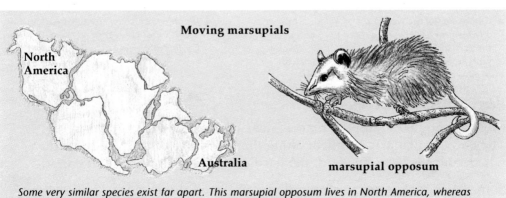

Some very similar species exist far apart. This marsupial opposum lives in North America, whereas most marsupilas live in Australia. This shows that continents which are now far apart were once part of the same giant land mass.

Earthquakes
The great plates

The twelve giant **plates** of rock which make up the Earth's crust fit together like pieces of a jigsaw puzzle. The plates can carry land or oceans, and many carry both.

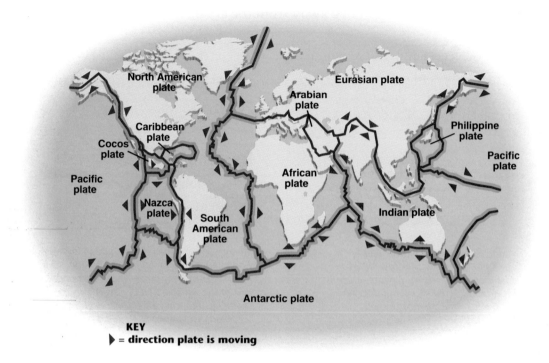

KEY
▶ = direction plate is moving

▲ *California, on the west coast of America, has a **transform fault** running through it, called the San Andreas fault. Over the last 50 million years, there has been about 5,000 kilometres of movement along the San Andreas fault.*

▲ *Japan, which suffers frequent earthquakes, is in a **subduction zone** at the edge of the Pacific plate.*

Earthquake zones

Most earthquakes happen in areas near where the Earth's plates meet. They are particularly frequent along the boundary of the Pacific Plate, which touches New Zealand, the Far East and North and South America.

Some earthquakes are so strong they can be felt thousands of kilometres away in different continents. An earthquake in Bolivia, South America, was felt by people in Toronto, 6,000 kilometres north.

The Earth's plates are constantly moving. Some plates move more quickly than others. They move in three main ways: away from each other at **mid-ocean ridges**, towards each other at **subduction zones**, or in different directions next to each other, at **transform faults**.

▶ *Where two plates are moving apart under the Atlantic Ocean, molten rock has pushed up to form a **mid-ocean ridge** of new crust. The crust spreads away from the ridge, and the ocean basin widens.*

▶ *As the sea-floor widens at the mid-ocean ridge, the other edge of the plate is forced down beneath the plate next to it at a **subduction zone**. The sinking rock melts and often causes earthquakes and volcanoes.*

▶ *At a **transform fault**, the plates can rub smoothly against each other for years. But if the plates jam together they can get stuck, and stress builds up. Eventually the plates 'snap free' with a jerk, and this jerk is an earthquake.*

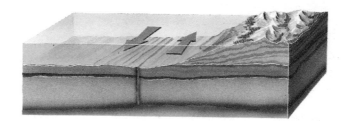

Inside an earthquake

When a crustal rock fractures it sends out shock waves in all directions. The source of these waves is called the **focus** of the earthquake. The point on the surface above the focus is the **epicentre**.

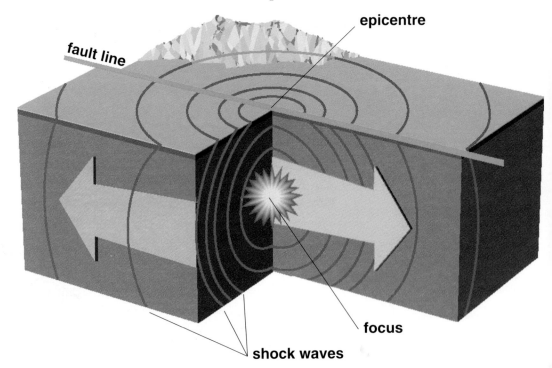

epicentre

fault line

focus

shock waves

Types of waves

There are three sorts of shock waves which radiate out from the earthquake's centre.

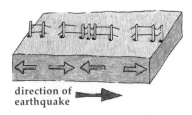

direction of earthquake

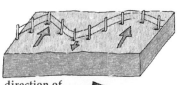

direction of earthquake

direction of earthquake

▲ *P-waves (pressure or primary waves) cause back and forth movement in the direction of the wave.*

▲ *S-waves, (shear or secondary waves) move back and forth at right angles to the direction of the wave.*

▲ *Surface waves cause ripples in the ground as they move outwards in a circular path at the surface.*

Measuring earthquakes

The **Richter scale** was introduced in 1935 by an American scientist, Dr Charles F. Richter. It is a way of measuring the energy that an earthquake releases at its focus. The amount of damage an earthquake causes depends on how close its focus is to the Earth's surface, and whether the affected areas are highly populated. Every year, seismographs around the world record 300,000 earthquakes, most of them between 3 and 8 on the Richter scale.

The **Mercalli scale** describes the actual damage caused by an earthquake. It is not precise like the Richter scale, but describes the sort of damage that people actually see and feel during an earthquake.

Mercalli scale	Richter scale	Damage caused
1	3	**very slight:** detected by instruments only
2	3–3.4	**feeble:** lights swing from ceilings
3	3.5–4	**slight:** parked cars rock slightly
4	4.1–4.4	**moderate:** windows rattle
5	4.5–4.8	**rather strong:** windows break
6	4.9–5.4	**strong:** trees sway, walls crack
7	5.5–6	**very strong:** buildings crack
8	6.1–6.5	**destructive:** some walls collapse, statues fall over
9	6.6–7	**ruinous:** heavy damage to buildings, ground cracks
10	7.1–7.3	**disastrous:** most buildings destroyed, landslides
11	7.4–8.1	**very disastrous:** few brick structures left standing
12	>8.1	**catastrophic:** ground heaves in waves, total devastation

Detecting earthquakes

Many earthquakes cause enormous natural disasters. In the last hundred years, one million people have died in earthquakes. Much effort is put in to detecting earthquakes in advance, so that people can be evacuated from the affected areas.

Scientists use instruments called **seismographs** to detect the tremors in the ground which happen all year round. A seismograph is a very sensitive microphone which can hear sound waves travelling through the Earth. During an earthquake, the sound waves detected can be used to measure the waves of energy radiating from the earthquake's epicentre. A sensitive seismograph can magnify a tiny tremor a million times. The tremor shows up as a wiggle in a line that a pen traces on a turning drum. The stronger the tremor, the greater the wiggle.

◀ *This seismograph is near the San Andreas fault in California USA. It has recorded four small tremors.*

Before an earthquake there is often a series of **foreshocks**, or minor tremors. These can signal (and even cause) an oncoming earthquake, and are often followed by a quiet period with no tremors or shocks. After the earthquake, there can be a series of **aftershocks**. The earth keeps trembling, rather as a bell can be heard to 'ring' even after it has stopped chiming. The aftershocks can continue for several days.

Changes in the natural world can often signal that an earthquake is on its way. Snakes have been known to move out of their underground nests, even in bitter winter weather, just before earthquakes. Animals can notice tiny vibrations and gases escaping from the Earth long before humans. Their unusual behaviour, such as suddenly running about in different directions, can signal an oncoming earthquake. Also, changing water levels in deep wells, or water jumping straight out of the Earth can all indicate underground upheavals.

Satellites

One of the most important satellites circling the world today is a tiny globe that looks like an enlarged golf ball. Only 61 centimetres in diameter but weighing 406 kilograms, LAGEOS (Laser Geodynamic Satellite) has been in orbit, 6,000 km from Earth, since the 1970s. It is designed to measure the distance between particular spots on different crustal plates using lasers. LAGEOS' surface, which is made up of 426 prisms, reflects the laser back to earth. The time taken for the laser beam to reach LAGEOS and return to earth discloses any change in the position of the Earth's plates, even when the change is only a few centimetres. The bigger the change in the distance between the plates, the greater the danger of earthquakes.

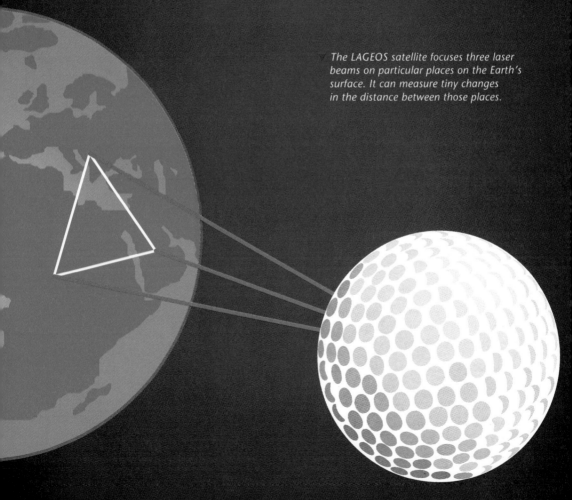

The LAGEOS satellite focuses three laser beams on particular places on the Earth's surface. It can measure tiny changes in the distance between those places.

The first earthquake recorder was invented by a Chinese philosopher called Zhang Heng in 132 AD. Inside an urn he dangled a pendulum, which was connected by moveable horizontal rods to a ring of eight open-mouthed dragon heads on the outside of the urn. Each mouth contained a ball. When an earthquake moved the pendulum, one of the balls fell into the open mouth of an earthenware toad, a ring of which were around the bottom of the urn. Then Zhang knew the direction the earthquake had originated from – but not its strength.

WARNING!
Earthquake Precautions
In a building
- ❑ stay indoors, away from glass
- ❑ go to ground floor or cellar if possible
- ❑ make sure there are plenty of exits
- ❑ get under a table which will give protection and an air space
- ❑ do not go in lifts

In a car
- ❑ stop as quickly as you can
- ❑ stay in the car
- ❑ crouch on the floor below seat level

Outdoors
- ❑ lie flat on the ground
- ❑ do not try to run
- ❑ keep away from tall buildings and trees
- ❑ do not go underground
- ❑ on a hillside, get to the top

◀ *These precautions are listed in survival manuals, but similar notices are found in areas prone to earthquakes.*

Famous earthquakes

San Francisco, USA, 1906

California is an earthquake zone because it straddles the San Andreas Fault, a 32 kilometre deep crack in the Earth's crust that runs half the length of the state. Somewhere in California, tremors are felt almost every day.

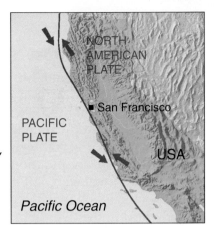

▲ San Andreas fault, 450 kilometres south of San Francisco.

On 18 April 1906, the edge of the Pacific Plate jolted northward six metres when its neighbouring American Plate gave way to its pressure. A police sergeant in San Francisco saw the earthquake approaching as the road rose and fell in huge waves. Buildings collapsed, gas pipes cracked and burst into flame, starting fires that lasted three days. Water pipes had fractured, leaving firefighters helpless. As there were many wooden buildings the fires completely destroyed the centre of the city.

The 1906 earthquake measured 8.25 Richters. The first shock lasted 48 seconds. Around 700 people were killed and hundreds more were injured.

The 1906 San Francisco earthquake was one of the most famous of the twentieth century. But it was by no means the most destructive, or the most powerful.

▶ The modern Transamerica building in San Francisco has an unusual pyramid design to prevent it collapsing in an earthquake.

T'ang-Shan, China, 1976

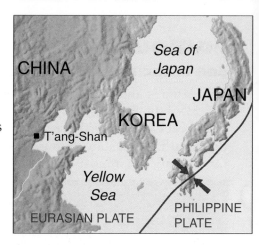

The earthquake which hit T'ang-Shan on 28 July 1976 measured 8.2 Richters, slightly less than the 1906 San Francisco earthquake. But the damage it caused was far, far worse. 750,000 people were killed – half the city's population – and only a few buildings were left standing. Of all the people killed in earthquakes around the world in the twentieth century, half of them died at T'ang-Shan.

Strange red and white lights in the sky were seen just before the earthquake struck. When the shaking began, many people were catapulted into the air – some as high as two metres! People described the quaking as violent hammer-like blows coming from beneath the earth.

◀ Hiroshima, Japan, after an atom bomb had been dropped in 1945. People said that the 1976 earthquake made T'ang-Shan look like this.

The city was rebuilt on another site with buildings designed to resist earthquakes. Its parks, rather than its buildings, were placed above fault lines. By the early 1980s, all the survivors had returned and new arrivals meant that the population was back to its pre-disaster level.

Armenia, 1988

The strongest earthquake ever recorded occurred on 7 December 1988, when a shock of 9 Richters hit two towns in the former Soviet republic of Armenia. Leninakan and Sitak were almost completely wiped out, and 25,000 people were killed.

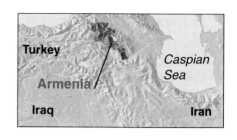

◀ Survivors amongst the ruins after the earthquake in Armenia.

Peru, 1970

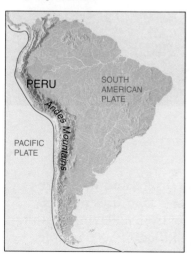

Earthquakes can have after-effects which can cause more damage than the earthquake itself. An earthquake measuring 7.8 Richters struck the Andes mountains in Peru on 31 May 1970. It caused a landslide of glacial ice and rock which dropped onto the towns of Yungay and Ramrahirca at 400 kilometres an hour. Both towns vanished in seconds. High above, a mountain lake burst its dam and sent water pouring into the valley. Altogether, 70,000 people died in the disaster.

Japan's earthquakes

Japan lies where the Eurasian plate meets the Pacific plate, which makes it a very active earthquake zone. It experiences a strong earthquake every 18 months and a major one every ten years. Until about 50 years ago, most Japanese people coped with the frequency of disaster by living in lightweight wooden houses as their ancestors had done. This meant that when an earthquake struck the houses collapsed, but as there were no heavy bricks or stones to fall down there was less risk of injury. The houses could also easily be rebuilt. But in the cities skyscrapers and buildings built of brick and concrete have changed skylines. A big shock wave takes only seconds to flatten these heavy buildings, and can cause many deaths and injuries as a result.

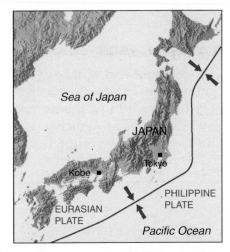

▶ Traditional lightweight wooden houses collapse easily in earthquakes. In many parts of the Japanese countryside people still live in this type of house.

Tokyo, Japan, 1923

On 1 September 1923, a massive earthquake struck Tokyo and the nearby port of Yokohama. Great chasms tore open the streets, and fires burned through 30,000 buildings. A fireball, breaking away from a blazing building, threw its victims high into the air. The earthquake killed 140,000 people.

Living in an earthquake zone

In the second half of the twentieth century, the Japanese people worked to reduce the risk of casualties and damage from earthquakes. Homes and offices were built on solid ground (away from the faults) and were capable of swaying during an earthquake. There are regular drill exercises for evacuation in schools and offices.

Kobe, Japan, 1995

When another huge earthquake struck Japan at Kobe, 400 kilometres south of Tokyo, on 17 January 1995, the damage was still enormous – but not nearly as great as it had been in Tokyo 72 years earlier. The 20-second earthquake, which measured 7.2 on the Richter scale and had hundreds of after-shocks, ripped up railway lines and motorways, ignited fires, blocked roads and ruptured water mains.

▲ Ordinary houses collapsed during the earthquake.

◄ The earthquake dominated the news all over the world.

Relief and rescue workers were seriously delayed because the city's streets were blocked by debris. Without water supplies readily available, helicopters drew millions of litres from the sea to douse the fire sweeping through the city. Nevertheless, 5,028 people were killed despite disaster plans and the help of modern technology.

Earthquakes and tsunamis

Earthquakes which occur beneath the sea bring another kind of danger. They can release huge sea waves known as **tsunamis**, which can cross an ocean at speeds as high as 750 kilometres per hour. Ships far from land are hardly affected by the waves because in the open sea, tsunamis are only a metre or so high. But where a tsunami meets the shore, the wave can be enormous. The biggest tsunami on record happened in 1771, when a wave 85 metres high struck the Japanese Ryukyu islands.

▼ If this wave was the largest ever recorded, a person would be about this big!

Earthquakes in Britain?

Even Britain has experienced earthquakes, although nothing to compare with those that happen on the edges of the great plates. The most severe earthquake to strike Britain shook towns from the east coast to Cheshire and down to the Isle of Wight on 22 April 1884. Several people died and 1,200 buildings were damaged. Minor shocks have also been felt in Nottinghamshire, Yorkshire, Herefordshire and Staffordshire. These shudders flow from mini-faults in the crust and seldom cause damage. One fault lies beneath the Caledonian Canal between Inverness and Fort William; the last tremor to be felt in the area occurred in 1988.

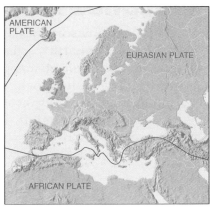

▲ The nearest earthquake zone to Great Britain is in the Mediterranean Sea.

Major earthquakes

Date	Place	Number killed
1556	China	830,000
1755	Lisbon, Portugal	50,000-100,000
1857	Tokyo, Japan	107,000
1906	San Francisco, USA	700
1920	Kansu, China	180,000
1923	Tokyo, Japan	140,000
1970	Peru	70,000
1976	Tangshan, China	600,000
1988	Armenia, USSR	25,000
1990	Gilan-Zanjan, Northern Iran	35,000
1995	Kobe, Japan	5,028

Frequency of earthquakes

Magnitude (Richters)	number per year (approx.)
1	700,000
2	300,000
3	300,000
4	50,000
5	6000
6	800
7	120
8	20
greater than 8	1 every few years

Volcanoes

Volcanoes are any sorts of natural openings
or fissures in the Earth's crust through which
hot molten rock, ash, steam, gas and other material
is spewed. The molten rock, called magma when
it's under the Earth's surface, is called **lava** as soon
as it has erupted through it. The word volcano
is also used to describe the cone of lava
and ash that builds up around the opening.

Tephra: lumps
of volcanic rock

Lava flow

Most of the volcano's ash
a chimney-like 'pipe' or vent
the material erupts. Far below
chamber of molten rock (magma)
dissolved gases. Gas bubbling out of the
magma keeps the vent open. Sometimes,
lava and other material may break through
further down the sides of the volcano and a
secondary or parasite cone is formed.

2 Hawaiian: mild and quiet

The runny, fluid lava of quiet volcanoes wells out smoothly from the ground and travels a long way before setting. This sort of lava flow does not block craters and so there is no pressure building up from inside. Hawaiian eruptions are also found in Iceland, but while in Hawaii the lava erupts through a central vent, in Iceland it usually pours out through cracks or fissures in the Earth's surface.

▲ *Runny lava pours into the Pacific Ocean from Mount Kilanea on the island of Hawaii.*

Parts of Northern Ireland and Scotland have a covering of basalt rock, produced by lava flows from ancient quiet volcanoes.

▲ *Runny basalt lava from ancient volcanoes has cooled to form spectacular natural columns. Giant's Causeway, County Antrim, Northern Ireland.*

27

3 Strombolian: thicker lava, explosive

Strombolian volcanoes erupt almost constantly with small explosions over a long period of time. There is usually only a little flow of lava. Sometimes small pockets of escaping gas force the molten lava to spray up like a fountain. Strombolian eruptions are named after Stromboli, an island volcano just north of Sicily in the Mediterranean Sea, which has been exploding almost without stopping for hundreds of years.

▶ *Eruption of Stromboli. The lava shower is 30 metres high.*

4 Peléean: thick lava, gigantic explosion, glowing cloud

In an explosive Peléean eruption a very hot cloud of gas and lava shoots out of the top or side of the volcano after an enormous explosion. The cloud of gas and red-hot solid rock fragments speed over the ground, destroying everything in its path. Peléean volcanoes are named after Mount Pelée in Martinique in the Caribbean.

◀ *This photograph of an eruption of Mount Pelée in Martinque was taken in 1902. It shows the 'nuée ardent' which destroyed the town of St Pierre.*
(See page 34)

Volcano shapes

▶ Shield volcano

Named after the curved shields of ancient warriors, shield volcanoes are built of many outflows of runny lava. Although they are not steep-sided, they can become very high mountains. Mauna Loa in Hawaii is an example of a shield volcano.

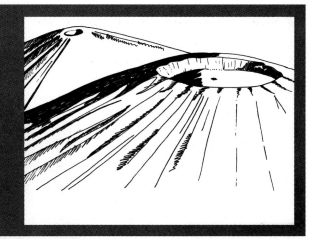

◀ Cinder cone volcano

Found where eruptions produce mainly tephra and ash and not much lava. Fragments of tephra fall on all sides of the vent creating a steep slope. They do not reach heights of more than 1500 metres. Mount Paricutin in Mexico is a good example.

▶ Composite or strato volcano

Composite volcanoes are more symmetrical than cinder cones and steeper than shields. The slopes are formed by a build-up of alternate layers of lava and tephra. They are the most spectacular volcanoes to look at. Mount Fuji in Japan is a composite volcano.

Benefits of volcanoes

Volcanic eruptions in populated areas can cause massive loss of life, and are greatly feared as a result. However, the energy within the earth has positive consequences, too. Probably its greatest use is in producing electricity. The whole of Iceland, a highly volcanic island in the north Atlantic, is powered by **geo-thermal** energy.

In addition, volcanic soils are some of the richest and most fertile. Lava creates basalt rock for building and pumice stone for the bathroom. In the Azores, the Atlantic islands west of Spain, villagers used to cook their food in hot holes dug in the ground or boiled in pots set in steaming, yellowish sulphur pools. And in places as far apart as New Zealand, Japan, Iceland and the US, hot springs from underwater basins produce natural **geysers** leaping high into the air, which have become tourist attractions.

▲ *This natural thermal lake is full of hot water. Note the rising steam.*

▲ *A geyser is a powerful hot spring.*

Tree rings and volcanoes

The huge amounts of dust which a massive volcanic eruption spews out into the atmosphere can affect growth of plants and trees all over the world. Tree rings, which can be counted to tell the age of the tree, also show when the tree grew less than usual. Narrow rings found in oak trees in Ireland, Germany, and America all record low growth in 208 BC, thought to be the time of an enormous Chinese volcano which caused massive loss of life.

Famous eruptions
Pompeii, Italy, 79 AD

One of the most famous volcanic eruptions happened nearly 2,000 years ago. This particular volcano is remembered because it preserved an ancient city whilst it destroyed it.

On 24 August 79 AD, Pompeii, a prosperous Roman town in southern Italy, was destroyed when the nearby volcano Vesuvius erupted. Within minutes 20,000 people were embedded in the falling cloud of black ash. Many others choked to death on poisonous gases that swirled through the town. Hot rocks and stones rained down and earthquakes shook the area for days.

It happened so quickly that people's postures – sitting or crouched on floors – were preserved for centuries. Fifteen hundred years later, pieces of jewellery, coins and the remains of a wall led excavators to Pompeii's ruins, buried beneath 18 metres of ash. But it was not until the late nineteenth century that serious work began to uncover the town – and archaeologists are still working on it.

▲ If they hadn't been preserved by the ash, these columns might have crumbled away.

▶ If this arrow represents the depth of ash which buried Pompeii, a person would be this big! ▼

Plaster casts were taken of cavities left by decomposing bodies, some of them with expressions of fear etched on their faces. They are a macabre part of the ruins, which show us how the people of Pompeii lived during the time of the Roman Empire.

▲ Pompeii's arena. Mount Vesuvius is in the background.

Krakatoa, Indonesia, 1883

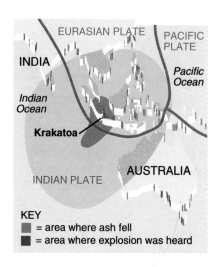

KEY
- = area where ash fell
- = area where explosion was heard

Another famous volcanic eruption was on the Indonesian island of Krakatoa. Having not erupted for 200 years, in the summer of 1883 there was a series of underground crashes and roars. These explosions went on for months, and people on the nearby islands of Java and Sumatra became used to them. But eventually sea water poured into Krakatoa's magma chamber. The intense heat instantly turned the water to steam, and the island blew itself apart on 27 August. The bang – said to be the loudest sound ever made in the world – awoke Australians 3,000 kilometres away, and could be heard on Rodriguez Island 4,800 kilometres across the vast Indian Ocean.

Although Krakatoa was uninhabited, its tremendous explosion created 40 metre high waves, or tsunamis, that swept away between 30,000 and 50,000 people on the two neighbouring islands. Molten lava blown up from Krakatoa dropped as fizzing rocks into the sea. Debris and ashes cascaded from a column of black smoke which rose 80 kilometres into the sky. Three hundred kilometres away people saw day become night as the ash obscured the sunlight. The ash was later carried as dust around the world, marking its progress by producing brilliant sunsets, seen as far away as London. Ash-filled clouds reduced sunshine and affected crops all over the world. There were high tides around the coasts of the Americas, and the level of the English Channel was higher than usual. But the most dramatic effect of the eruption was that the island completely changed shape.

▲ Before the explosion of 1883.

▲ After the event.

▲ The formation of a new volcano.

Mount St Helens, USA, 1980

Nowadays, we are able to detect when volcanoes are likely to erupt. When Mount St Helens in Washington State erupted in 1980, scientists who had been monitoring the underground activity beneath the mountain for a decade had been predicting an eruption. Nonetheless, one scientist, David Johnston, was killed by the eruption, because it was a different sort than had been expected.

The 2,900 metre high volcano had exploded five times in nearly 300 years, and had been active for at least 40,000 years. In 1980, a bulge was seen developing on its north face which grew to a kilometre across. One thousand people were evacuated from a 32 kilometre radius around the volcano. At breakfast time on 18 May, a small earthquake triggered a giant landslide which removed the entire north face of the volcano. This reduced pressure in the magma chamber (just like unscrewing a cola bottle) which lead to an enormous explosive eruption. The volcano blasted 430 metres off the mountain's top. A huge cloud rose (see page 26) and was carried 750 kilometres by winds to the states of Montana and Idaho. There, ash fell so deeply that snow ploughs were used to clear the blocked roads.

◀ *Before the 1980 eruption, Mount St Helens was a conical mountain. Now, inside the massive crater left behind, another 'plug' of lava has formed above the central vent.*

33

Mount Pelée, Martinique, 1902

The greatest volcanic disaster of the twentieth century happened on the West Indian island of Martinique on 8 May 1902, when Mount Pelée erupted. In just three minutes, more than 30,000 people died as a cloud of hot gas called a *nuée ardent* swept down the side of the volcano. The town of St Pierre was completely destroyed.

The people of St Pierre were not killed by the ash, but by the intense heat. The cloud of hot dust which burnt down the town melted forks, nails and glass bottles into strange shapes. There was only one survivor. A man called Cyparis had been jailed for murder and was awaiting execution. Because his dungeon-like cell was underground with only a small air vent, he was safe from the invading lava and ash. He was later reprieved, and spent his life travelling with a circus, telling his story.

In about 1470 BC, the Greek island of Santorini blew up, destroying the Bronze Age civilization of Minoa. The explosion is calculated to have been 120 times as powerful as the biggest nuclear weapon ever tested.

Volcanoes that:
- erupt fairly often are **active**.
- are non-active for many years between eruptions are **dormant**. Some volcanoes are dormant for hundreds of years.
- have long since stopped erupting are **extinct**.

The word 'volcano' comes from Vulcanus, the Roman god of fire. The ancient Romans believed that Vulcanus lived beneath a fiery island off Sicily which they called Vulcano.

Pumice stone is 80% air. It is created by frothy lava setting with bubbles of air still within it.

Major volcanic eruptions

470 BC	Santorini, Greece	island destroyed
79 AD	Pompeii, Italy	town buried under ash
1669	Etna, Sicily	20,000 dead
1783	Skaptar Jokul, Iceland	20% of population killed (9,000 people)
1794	Tunquraohua, Ecuador	40,000 killed, city of Riobemba destroyed
1883	Krakatoa, Java	up to 50,000 killed by tsunami
1902	Pelée, Martinique	up to 36,000 killed
1944	Paricutin, Mexico	3,500 killed, two towns buried in ash
1985	Nevado del Ruiz, Colombia	25,000 killed
1991	Mount Pinatubo, Philippines	400 killed

Storms

People often joke about how boring it is to talk about the weather. But in some parts of the world, weather can sweep away houses, lift lorries high up into the sky, and cause floods which wash away whole towns.

Hurricanes

A hurricane is an extremely violent storm. It begins as an intense area of low pressure. This area can be up to 500 kilometres across. Currents of hot, moist air rise from the tropical seas and begin to spin into the centre of the area of low pressure. As the speed of the spin increases, the storms move towards the north and south poles. A hurricane's wind speed can be up to 200 km per hour. When a hurricane meets the colder air from the polar region, the moisture in the hot air falls as heavy rain. Hurricanes spin anticlockwise in the northern hemisphere, and clockwise in the southern hemisphere.

▼ Inside a hurricane

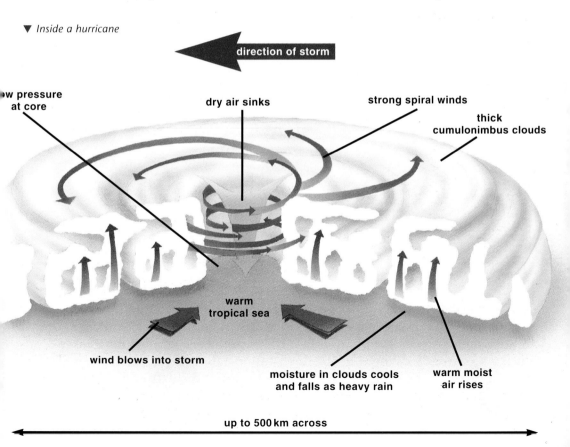

direction of storm

low pressure at core

dry air sinks

strong spiral winds

thick cumulonimbus clouds

warm tropical sea

wind blows into storm

moisture in clouds cools and falls as heavy rain

warm moist air rises

up to 500 km across

Hurricanes usually form in sub-tropical regions, just north or south of the equator. They begin over seas which have become warmer than 27°C. In the northern hemisphere the hurricane season is June to November, and in the southern hemisphere it is November to April. This type of storm is called a hurricane in the Caribbean and North Atlantic, but is known as a **typhoon** in the Far East, a **cyclone** around the Bay of Bengal, and as a **willy-willy** in northern Australia.

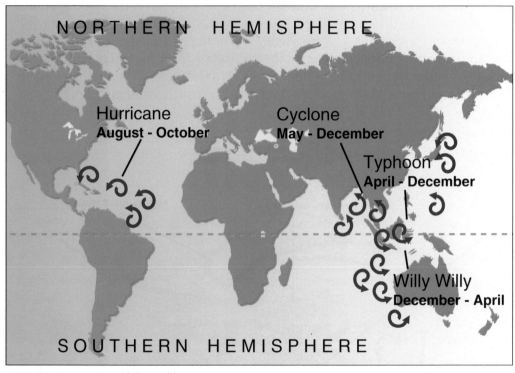

▲ Hurricane zones around the world.

If a hurricane strikes land it causes enormous damage. Sometimes whole towns and villages are wiped out. Once it is travelling over land, a hurricane loses its supply of moisture from the sea and begins to slow down, eventually dying. But the devastation caused by a hurricane is not only a result of the speed of the wind, but also of the extremely heavy rains. Hurricanes can also cause massive tidal waves called **storm surges**, some of which are as high as eight metres, which can sweep inland, washing away everything in their path.

The eye of the storm

In the centre of every hurricane there is an area of very low pressure with light winds and clear skies. This is the **eye of the storm**. Because a hurricane is circular in shape, the winds blow in opposite directions on either side of the eye. People caught in a hurricane find that after the winds have howled for several hours from one direction they die down, creating a deceptive calm that is really only a brief interval as the eye passes overhead. After an hour or less, the winds on the other side of the hurricane arrive, blowing just as violently as they did from the opposite direction.

◀ *Hurricane seen from space. The hole in the middle of the circular cloud is the eye.*

The Beaufort Scale

In 1805, Admiral Sir Francis Beaufort worked out a scale for measuring wind speed at sea. His scale is still used today, but has been altered for use on land. According to the Beaufort Scale, the official measurement for wind speeds, a hurricane is born when gales reach 120 kph. Sir Francis described a hurricane as a wind 'such as no canvas could withstand'.

Force 1 *(2-5 kph)* *Light air*

Smoke drifts but wind vanes do not move.

Force 2 *(6-11 kph)* *Light breeze*

Leaves rustle and wind vanes move.

Force 3 *(12-19 kph)* *Gentle breeze*

Leaves and small twigs move.

Force 4 *(20-29 kph)* *Moderate breeze*

Dust raised, small branches move

Force 5 *(30-39 kph)* *Fresh breeze*

Small trees with leaves sway.

Force 6 *(40-50 kph)* *Strong breeze*

Large branches move. Phone wires whistle.

Force 7 *(51-61 kph)* *Near gale*

Whole trees sway.

Force 8 *(62-74 kph)* *Gale*

Twigs break off trees. Walking difficult.

Force 9 *(75-87 kph)* *Strong gale*

Chimney pots brought down.

Force 10 *(88-102kph)* *Storm*

Damage to buildings. Trees uprooted.

Force 11 *(103-120kph)* *Violent storm*

Widespread damage.

Force 12 *(over120kph)* *Hurricane*

Whole area devastated.

The British hurricane, 1987

The worst British storm of the 20th century arrived unexpectedly on 15 October 1987, when hurricane-force winds reaching 170 kph caused at least seventeen deaths and left a swathe of destruction across the south east of England.

Thousands of trees were uprooted, blocking roads and railway lines, and many buildings were badly damaged. Electricity supplies were cut off in some areas. In Sussex, a ship was washed ashore. Every London hospital casualty ward was filled with victims of flying roof slates, road accidents and falling trees. Firefighters answered thousands of emergency calls during that disastrous day.

◀ *In this forest in Suffolk, only one in ten trees was left standing after the 1987 hurricane.*

Weather satellites

Weather changes are almost always seen well in advance, as temperatures and cloud patterns can be photographed by satellites in space. However, mistakes still happen: the 1987 British hurricane was not forecast at all, and caught the country unawares.

▶ *This photograph of a hurricane was taken by a satellite.*

North Atlantic hurricane zone

Every year, six or more hurricanes develop in the warm, tropical North Atlantic. Two or three of these cause havoc as they pass over the Caribbean islands or strike the coasts of the United States and Central America. More than one million people have died in the hurricanes of the North Atlantic in the last hundred years.

▶ *These beach-side houses have been hit by an enormous hurricane and lashed by the sea.*

Hurricane Fifi, 1974

Most hurricanes which threaten the American coasts are given a name by meteorologists, who track the paths of storms using weather satellites. The names chosen are in alphabetical order. The hurricane that burst upon Central America on 19 September 1974 was called 'Fifi'. Fifi produced a death toll of 10,000 as it tore through Honduras, Belize, Guatemala and El Salvador. Tidal waves raced inland. In a few hours, 60,000 people lost their homes. Almost all the crops in Honduras

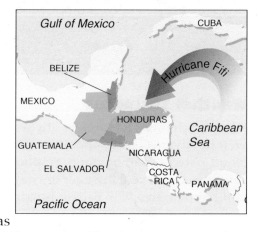

were destroyed as thousands of square kilometres of land were swamped by the sea and torrential rain. In the Honduran town of Cruz Laguna, every house was washed out to sea, and almost its whole population of 1,500 was killed. After the storm, rescuers found survivors still clinging to tree tops.

Hong Kong's emergency typhoon procedure

In Hong Kong, hurricane-force storms are called **typhoons**, from the Cantonese words *daai fung*, meaning *great wind*. Hong Kong has a population of six million, and the Far East's most envied early warning storm systems.

Aid agencies and the emergency services work together and act quickly whenever there is a threat of a typhoon. Warnings are widely broadcast, and there is a well-rehearsed emergency procedure.

WARNING!

Typhoon Precautions

→ Get out of the typhoon's path if you can.

→ Listen for the 24-hour advance warning.

→ Keep away from the coast and from river banks.

→ Board up windows and secure any objects outdoors that might blow away.

TYPHOON SIGNAL NO. 3 IS HOISTED

▲ *In Hong Kong, signs like these warn people of a typhoon well in advance.*

Blood donor units and social services prepare to deal with casualties and people made homeless. When the alarms sound, temporary shelters are prepared, and thousands of meals are ready for distribution. The Red Cross keeps clothing and blankets for people who have been evacuated. Teams of rescuers are on standby, as are engineers to tackle landslides and damaged roads, and to maintain electricity generators. Helicopters are ready to rescue casualties. Hong Kong is probably the safest place in the world to be caught in a hurricane.

How a cyclone changed a government

The disastrous cyclone of 1970 which hit the small country of Bangladesh, then called East Pakistan, not only caused devastation. It also caused a major political upheaval.

Cyclone Opal, 1970

Bangladesh lies in the low-lying area around the mouth of the Ganges, where the river splits into many tributaries. This sort of area is called a **delta**.

The country is used to the annual season of cyclones which blow in from the Bay of Bengal. But the storm which struck on **13 February 1970** was the biggest disaster ever to hit the tiny country, one of the poorest places on Earth.

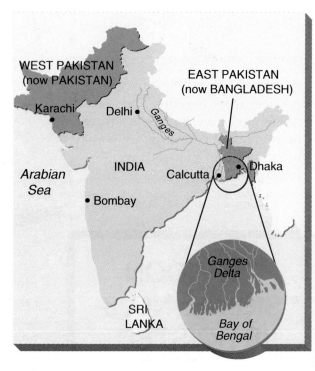

The gathering storm had been spotted hours earlier by weather satellites. But few of East Pakistan's population of 120 million heard the warnings broadcast on the radio.

The cyclone flattened buildings on the outlying islands. Then a storm surge raced through the network of rivers, accompanied by pouring rain. In vain, people tried to shelter upstairs, as thousands were carried away and drowned by the flood. But it was five whole days and nights before any emergency help reached the survivors.

Emergency supplies gathered by relief agencies piled up in Dacca, the capital. But there was no transport to move them across the floods to the outlying islands. The government of West Pakistan was slow to help its devastated province. Meanwhile, chaos increased in the Ganges delta as fresh water supplies ruptured and disease spread.

42

The cyclone had killed 500,000 people. Two million people were injured or made homeless. Crops were swamped by the floods. The destruction covered an area as big as Greater London.

▶ *A Bangladeshi family waiting to be rescued, having been flooded out of their home*

The consequences of the cyclone

In 1947, the country had been divided into East and West Pakistan, which were thousands of kilometres apart. East Pakistan became the independent nation of Bangladesh in 1971 partly because aid to the survivors was delayed by its rulers in West Pakistan. The party which won East Pakistan's next general election was quick to declare the country's independence. After a nine month civil war against West Pakistan, the independent nation of Bangladesh finally emerged.

Cyclones continue to strike Bangladesh. Since 1970, the country has set up an early warning system using weather satellites which gives 24 hours notice of approaching cyclones. Thousands of palm trees have been planted along the coast to act as a massive wind barrier, and many shelters have been built. On 29 April 1991, a cyclone with winds of up to 300 kph swept into the delta. But, warned in advance, hundreds of thousands of islanders were evacuated. Despite all this, 38,000 Bangladeshis died.

Tornadoes

Tornadoes, like hurricanes, are whirling masses of air with intensely low pressure at the centre. But with winds travelling at up to 350 kph, they are the most destructive weather patterns in the world.

Tornadoes occur when low level warm, moist air meets high level cold, dry air.

A tornado is rarely more than 800 metres across, but can travel up to 500 kilometres at a speed of 50-65 kph. Accurate measurement of the speed of the winds are difficult to obtain, because a tornado can wrench the instrument used for measuring wind speed from its stand!

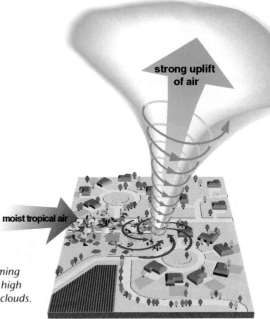

high cold air

strong uplift of air

moist tropical air

▶ Warm moist air spins at high speed as it rises, forming a funnel which sucks in more air. When it hits the high cold air, the moisture condenses and forms heavy clouds.

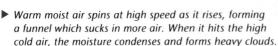

Cold dry air

UNITED

Warm moist air

STATES

Gulf of Mexico

Pacific Ocean

Tornado zones

The world's most destructive tornadoes are common in the American Midwest during March and April, when warm moist air flows north from the Gulf of Mexico and meets cold dry air, which flows over the top of it. They are often known as 'twisters', or 'Black Cobra', because the way they move and strike is like a snake.

What a tornado does

An approaching tornado appears as a tall, funnel-shaped cloud, which can be white brown or black, looming out of a dark indigo sky. There is often heavy rain, thunder and lightning. As the tornado comes nearer a deep roar can be heard, which gets louder and louder. At sea, tornadoes create huge funnels of water.

Tornadoes act like massive vacuum cleaners, and may suck up anything in their paths, including people, animals, vehicles, and even small buildings, which are carried hundreds of metres and then sent plummeting to the ground.

Although the damage can be severe and people may be killed, the track of the tornado is narrow. Roofs of houses on one side of a road can be lifted off, while those on the other side are untouched.

◄ With wind speeds of up to 350 km per hour, tornadoes cause terrible destruction and are greatly feared.

Tornado spring

In April 1974, more than a hundred tornadoes crossed the United States from the south to as far north as Ontario in Canada. 329 people were killed, and thousands more were injured. Cars, lorries and even trains were overturned as one after another the tornadoes moved north.

45

British tornadoes

Tornadoes are rare in Britain. When they do occur they lack the power of those in North America. In 1965, a tornado struck Swansea where it overturned cars and caravans, and sucked up a waterspout 60 metres high as it crossed a river. In January 1974 another hit Crewkerne, Somerset, damaging 90 houses, ripping the roof from a police station and smashing several greenhouses. In August that year several waterspouts about 300 metres high were seen in the English Channel.

WARNING!

Tornado Precautions

▶ Take shelter in a solid structure, like a cellar or cave. If you have no cellar, go to the centre of the lowest floor and shelter under heavy furniture. Keep away from windows.

▶ Close doors and windows on the side facing the tornado. Open those on the opposite side. This prevents the wind getting in and lifting off the roof, and will equalise the pressure to prevent the house from exploding.

▶ Do not stay in cars or caravans. When you see a tornado approaching, get out of the way. Take shelter in a ditch, lie flat and cover your head with your hands.

Index

Italic page numbers indicate where there is a diagram.